To everyone who reads this book – I hope that this
will help you on your own money journey.
D.M.

I hope you all enjoy reading this book and continue to be curious.
Thank you to designers Faith and Mitch, and to my agent Juliette
for bringing me into contact with this book. It was a great honour.
And thank you to my family and my little one, Ample.
H.H.

First published in Great Britain 2023 by Red Shed, part of Farshore
An imprint of HarperCollins*Publishers*
1 London Bridge Street, London SE1 9GF
www.farshore.co.uk

HarperCollins*Publishers*
Macken House, 39/40 Mayor Street Upper, Dublin 1, D01 C9W8

Text copyright © Deborah Meaden 2023
Deborah Meaden has asserted her moral rights.
Illustrations © HarperCollins*Publishers* 2023
Illustrated by Hao Hao.
Photograph of Deborah Meaden by Charles Glover.

ISBN 978 0 00 852090 8
Printed and bound in Italy.
001

A CIP catalogue record for this title is available from the British Library.

Stay safe online. Any website addresses listed in this book are correct at the time of going
to print. However, Farshore is not responsible for content hosted by third parties. Please
be aware that online content can be subject to change and websites can contain content that
is unsuitable for children. We advise that all children are supervised when using the internet.

Farshore takes its responsibility to the planet and its inhabitants very seriously.
We aim to use papers from well-managed forests run by responsible suppliers.

Little EXPERTS

DEBORAH MEADEN

WHY MONEY MATTERS

ILLUSTRATED BY
HAO HAO

RED SHED

INTRODUCTION

Have you ever heard the saying 'money makes the world go round'? Well, when I was very little, I imagined someone putting money into a machine that would spin the world round and round, a bit like the slot machines you can play at the seaside.

Of course, that seems silly now, but to a little girl with a big imagination, that was exactly what I thought, and it fascinated me. I had no idea what money even meant, except that it made the world turn round like a ballerina in a music box.

It became more real when I heard my parents talk about it, a lot . . . sometimes because we didn't have enough money to buy the things we wanted.

When I was older, they started giving me a small amount of money each week. Sometimes this wasn't enough for the things I wanted. They explained that if I wanted more, I could do something to 'earn' it. I didn't know then, but they were teaching me the value of money . . . a lesson that I still carry with me today.

I made my first money when I was seven years old selling flowers from the garden. Having my own money felt good and meant I could do what I wanted with it. At eight I had saved enough to buy myself a silver horseshoe charm for my bracelet. I soon realised this was only the start, and that if I wanted to add more charms, then I'd need to keep saving.

Since then I have spent my life owning businesses that make money. The money they make is used to pay the people who work there, to buy things from other businesses and people (so they too can make money), and to pay me enough money to be able to do the things I want to do.

Money may not literally make the world go round, but it is a very big part of the human world we all live in now. In this book we are going to take a fascinating journey to discover where money came from and why, and how it shapes the world we live in today, so that you can become a money expert.

COWS, KINGS AND POTATO MASHERS

Money is what people use to buy things. Before money, people would swap things they had for things they wanted. This is called bartering, but it didn't work very well . . .

Imagine you were a baker and you wanted meat. If the butcher didn't want your bread, then you wouldn't be able to swap! Or, imagine you had a cow and were happy to swap it for 300 loaves, but you didn't want them all at once! How did you know the baker would keep their promise to give you all 300 loaves?

To make things simpler, people started to use things that were easy to carry around. They were objects that were hard to find or make, which made them valuable. People would swap these for things they wanted, when they wanted them. This was the start of money and included shells and beads.

The Bafia people sometimes used iron potato mashers in exchange for things they wanted.

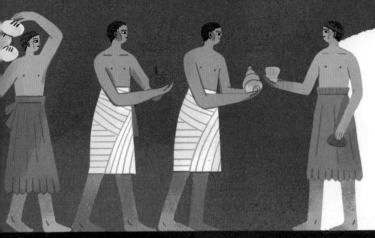

But there were still problems! Imagine you had lots of people working for you and you gave people different sized shells. Would that be fair?

Luckily, the Royal Palace in Mesopotamia came up with a clever answer about 5,000 years ago. They used standard weights of silver to measure wages, so workers could be paid fairly and buy what they needed. However, the value wasn't in the silver. Instead, the government ordered its people to TRUST that it was worth what they said it was worth, and they did!

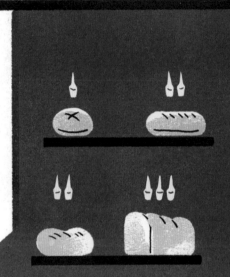

When the workers went to the baker with this new silver money, for example, they could see how many pieces of silver they would need for their loaf, because the baker could set a price.

It doesn't matter what shape, size or colour actual money is. It works because people BELIEVE in its value and TRUST they will be able to swap it for the things they want.

SHINY SHELLS TO METAL COINS

Money used to look very different around the world. People used objects, such as shells. But . . . things that were valuable in one place because they were hard to find, might have no value somewhere else because they were everywhere. Say you lived by the sea and could easily find shells, you wouldn't think they were valuable, would you?

So about 3,000 years ago in a kingdom in Lydia (in what we now call Turkey), someone came up with a brilliant idea . . . a token made from electrum (a mix of gold and silver) that everyone would recognise and know the value of. In other words, a coin!

Soon coins were used across the world. They were made of different metals and didn't look the same, but each was given a standard value that would be recognised far and wide.

Coins did another clever thing too. Different coins could be given different values, so when you paid for something, you could make up exactly the right amount of money. Or if you didn't have the exact money, you could hand over too much and get some coins back as change.

A coin factory is called a mint. British coins used to be roughly round gold or silver discs. Gold and silver were valuable, so people would sometimes cheat and chop bits off to melt down and sell on.

In 1696, Isaac Newton became Warden of the Royal Mint in London and decided that all coins must be made perfectly round with ridged edges. This made them harder for people to copy or chop!

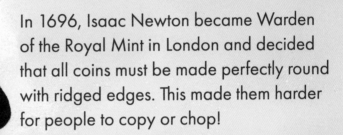

Even mints make mistakes and it can be fun to see if you can find any, such as the 2008 20p coins that have no date on.

Today, coins are made from metal that is melted, made into bars called ingots, and rolled into sheets. Blank coins are then punched out, cleaned and stamped twice.

CHALLENGE: *Two 1ps weigh the same as one 2p. Guess how much money you have in a handful of 1p and 2p coins, just by weighing a 1p and then weighing the whole handful.*

FOLLOW THE PAPER TRAIL

Coins were doing a great job but if you had lots of them, they were VERY heavy! Another solution was needed . . .

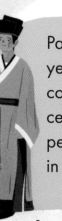

Paper certificates were used in China over 1,000 years ago. Merchants didn't feel safe carrying coins and valuables, so they started writing certificates promising to pay later. But some people didn't pay and the emperor stepped in to create the first legal banknote.

These banknotes were safer because the Chinese government promised they could be exchanged for coins.

Explorer Marco Polo told Europeans about paper banknotes in 1296 but they didn't catch on . . . people didn't believe they could be worth anything! Over 350 years later, in 1661, Sweden issued its first banknotes.

At first people wouldn't use Swedish banknotes until a group of trusted men had signed each one.

Eventually, people began to trust paper money and see how much better and safer it was.

In 1833 banknotes became 'legal tender' in England and Wales, which meant they had to be accepted by law if you wanted to buy something with them.

The words 'I promise to pay the bearer on demand' still appear on British banknotes today. See if you can find this.

British banknotes were still partly written by hand until they became fully printed in 1853.

Now money is made using machines. British banknotes are printed on a type of plastic so that they last longer. Huge rolls are fed into presses and printed to make the notes difficult to copy. Each banknote takes up to six weeks to make.

Old British paper notes were composted and spread onto farmers' fields. Think how many millions of pounds potatoes and carrots were growing in! Today plastic notes can be recycled and made into things such as plant pots.

We now call the paper money and coins we use 'currency', and many currencies are used around the world.

HIDDEN MONEY

Today we call coins and notes 'currency', but what about the ways that we can pay for things without using these? What about the money that we CAN'T see?

BANK

Let's start with credit cards. A bank will give people a credit card with an amount of money they can spend up to on it. It can be used to pay for things in a shop or online. It really should be called a borrowing card because we are actually borrowing money!

CREDIT CARD

At least some of the money must be paid back every month. We will pay extra for the money we haven't paid back – it's called interest.

A debit card looks like a credit card but is very different. When someone buys something with a debit card, the bank takes the money straight from the person's account and pays it to the shop or person they are buying from.

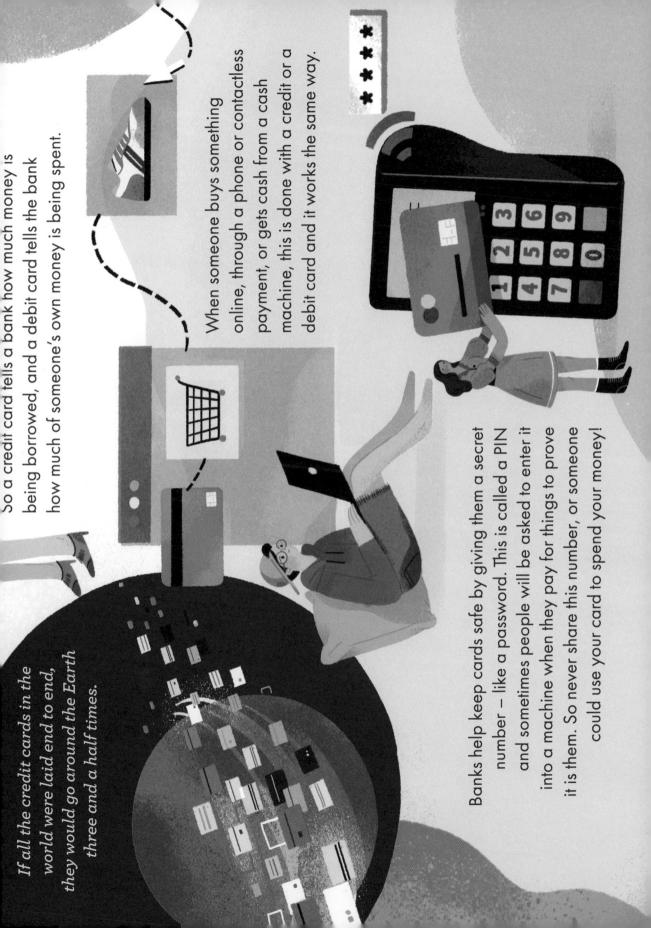

So a credit card tells a bank how much money is being borrowed, and a debit card tells the bank how much of someone's own money is being spent.

When someone buys something online, through a phone or contactless payment, or gets cash from a cash machine, this is done with a credit or a debit card and it works the same way.

If all the credit cards in the world were laid end to end, they would go around the Earth three and a half times.

Banks help keep cards safe by giving them a secret number – like a password. This is called a PIN and sometimes people will be asked to enter it into a machine when they pay for things to prove it is them. So never share this number, or someone could use your card to spend your money!

WHAT ARE BANKS?

Banks look after our money, help us buy things with credit and debit cards, and lend money. You can also tell your bank to take money from you to pay to someone (called a transfer).

Remember, money doesn't have to be seen. When you spend £5 using a card or transfer, don't imagine someone running from your bank to the shop to hand over a £5 note. Instead imagine numbers.

When you spend money, the numbers in your account go down because you have given that money to someone else, and when you save the numbers go up. Banks keep a record of the numbers.

Banking started just over 4,000 years ago, when priests in temples in Babylon looked after people's gold, lent money and kept records.

In Britain in the 1600s, people would hand gold to goldsmiths to keep safe. In return they received a note promising to pay up to the value of their gold 'on demand'. Goldsmiths would also lend money and keep valuables safe. Many became the first banks.

The UK government set up the Bank of England in 1694. Its job is to produce banknotes, keep an eye on things, such as card payments, and help keep the value of our money safe.

As part of the UK's wealth, it has around 400,000 gold bars. The keys to where they're kept are almost one metre long!

Banks are important today because they help move our money so we can buy, save and spend. They also move money around the world, which helps us buy and sell things to and from other countries.

HOW TO MAKE YOUR MONEY GROW

When we have more money than we need to spend, this is called savings. We can keep savings at home in a piggy bank or money box, or put them into a bank.

Banks want our money because they make money by lending ours to other people. So, if you have savings in a bank, they will pay you. This is called interest.

INTEREST

SAVINGS

BANK

BANK

If you need more money than you have, you could borrow some from a bank. You agree on how much and for how long.

This time you will have to pay the bank to use the money! This is also called interest.

Interest is the reward for savin or the cost of borrowing, so let see how this works . .

'Pygg' is an Old English word for a type of clay used to make pots and plates, including those used to keep money in. Over time the word became 'piggy bank' and they became the shape of a pig.

The bank sets something called an interest rate. This is how much they will pay you for every pound you save or how much they will charge you for every pound you borrow.

Let's say I am a saver. The bank agrees to pay 10% interest. I put £100 into my account. After a year they pay me 10% interest (£10). Now I have £110 . . . easy, right?

I decide to leave my £110 in the bank for another year. They then pay me 10% interest on £110 (£11), so at the end of year two I now have £121. This is called compound interest.

CHALLENGE:

You will need:
Two jars
25 tokens (e.g. buttons, jelly beans or even scraps of paper)

1. *Place two tokens in one jar every day for five days.*

2. *In the other jar, place two tokens every day for five days, PLUS one token for interest you are being paid by the bank every day.*

3. *On day five, count up the tokens in each jar. How many do you have?*

19

EARNING MONEY

Having your own money can feel good because it means you can save up to do the things you want. Maybe you want to give presents or buy yourself something. But how do you get it?

Friends and family may give you money for special occasions, such as birthdays, or maybe you get money every week called pocket money. You can also be given money as a reward for jobs that you do. This is called earnings.

There are lots of ways to earn money: running errands, washing cars, doing any sort of chore that someone will pay you to do . . . although it is also nice to do things just to be kind!

You can also earn money by asking your family to sell things that you no longer use, such as toys.

Did you know snake milking is a job! They 'milk' the poisonous venom from snakes for scientists to use to help people that have been bitten by deadly snakes.

The first money I ever earned was selling flowers from the garden.

When you get older you may work for a company who pays you regularly in what is called wages or a salary, or you may work for yourself and earn money from something you do or sell. What job do you think you'd like to do?

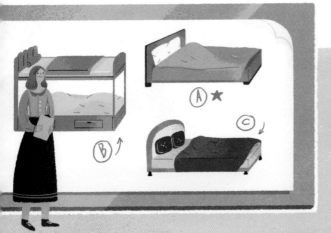

There is even a job being a professional sleeper! A hotel in Finland hired someone to sleep in a different bed every night to test how comfortable they were.

WHAT IS TAX?

Whatever job you decide to do, and whether you work for a company or for yourself (self-employed), you won't get to keep all of the money you earn. Surprise! Some of it goes to the government and this is called tax.

There are lots of different types of tax, but let's have a look at some of the main ones (income tax, sales tax and National Insurance). Income tax and National Insurance both come out of earnings and the amount someone pays depends on how much they earn.

What? That isn't fair! Or is it . . .? Do you go to school? Have you been to see a doctor or used the library? Is your rubbish collected? Does where you live have firefighters and police officers? All of these things (and lots more!) are paid for by the government from money they receive in taxes.

Some National Insurance money goes to help pay people when they are elderly, sick or do not have enough money to meet their needs.

If you're thinking that you won't have to pay tax for years, then you're wrong, because some of the things we buy have sales tax (called VAT) included in the price. So, if you use your pocket money to buy a toy from a shop, some of the money you pay will go to the government. You are already making a financial contribution to where you live!

PAY TAX

CHALLENGE:

Write a list of the places you go to or see every day. Then try to decide who pays for them to be built and looked after. Put a 'g' against all of the places you think are looked after by the government – then discuss with a grown-up.

LIBRARY

POLICE

NEEDS VS WANTS

How do you decide what to spend your money on? There are lots of things in life you might WANT (e.g. a games console) but do you really NEED them? Things you need are the things you must have to live your life (e.g. food). Wants are the things you can live without.

What can you see that are 'wants' and what are 'needs'?

The things you need should be bought first. Then, if there is money left, you can start to think about the things you want.

Think carefully when you want to buy something for yourself. If you buy something you will never use, it may mean that you can't buy something you really want later.

NEEDS

£10

£200

£60

Before you buy something, think hard about whether you are happy with it. Is it a fair price? Is it good quality? Has it been made in a way that is kind to people and the planet?

If there isn't anything you really want now, then save your money until there is.

Not everything you want has to cost money. You can always borrow or swap things with friends, and some of the best things in life are free.

One of the most expensive ice creams in the world cost $25,000 (about £20,000). It was sprinkled with edible gold and eaten with a gold and diamond spoon that could be taken home!

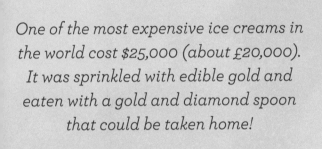

CHALLENGE: *Why not surprise your family and suggest a day out that doesn't cost much? Perhaps go for a walk, listen to a band in the park and take a picnic, or go to an event at the library? What's your plan?*

MONEY PLANS

Now we understand money and we know what we can do with it, we must use it wisely. And that needs a plan!

This sort of plan is called a budget and it is a way to make sure you have the money you need when you need it. A budget compares the money you have coming *in* with the money you have going *out*. If you have more money coming in than you need to spend, you can start thinking about the things you want to buy.

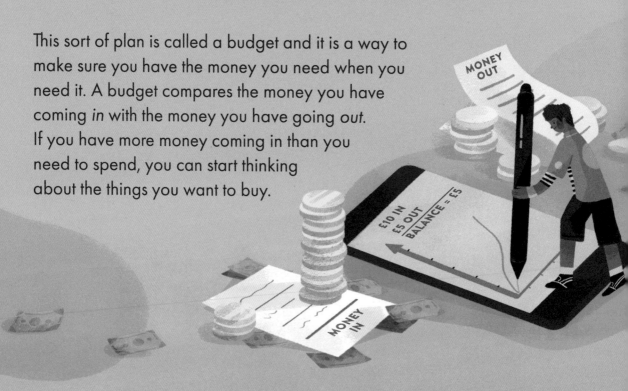

So far so good. BUT, what if you already know you will have to pay for something BIG in the future? A budget can help you look forward and work out how much money you need and when, so you can pay for that big thing when you have to.

Budgets help you buy the things you want. If you know what you must pay for, then you can start saving spare money for something special.

...ndreds of years ago, 'budget' used to mean a small bag that often carried money or ...portant papers. These papers were usually about money, and over time the papers themselves started to be called budgets.

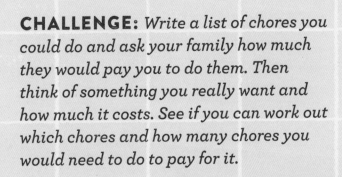

Money
Making
PLAN

🐶 £3
🚗 £6
🧹 £2
☕ £1

CHALLENGE: Write a list of chores you could do and ask your family how much they would pay you to do them. Then think of something you really want and how much it costs. See if you can work out which chores and how many chores you would need to do to pay for it.

PLAN

BILL

VAT

Next time you pull out a coin from your pocket, or if you are lucky enough to receive money as a present, you can think of the amazing journey money has made through history, and know that you are now ready for your own money journey.

GLOSSARY

ancient Romans – People who originated from Rome, Italy, and were part of an empire that began over 2,700 years ago and lasted for more than a thousand years.

Babylon – An ancient capital city of Mesopotamia.

Bafia people – A group of people who live in Cameroon, a country in West Africa.

contactless payment – A way of paying for things with a debit or credit card without needing to enter a PIN code.

entrepreneur – Someone who sets up their own business.

government – A group of people who make the laws and important decisions that affect people in a country or area.

interest rate – The amount you will be paid for your savings or charged to borrow money, shown as a percentage (e.g. 5%).

legal – Something that is covered by, or has something to do with, law (a set of rules that people have to follow).

merchants – People who buy goods and sell them to make money.

Mesopotamia – An area of land mainly around the Euphrates and Tigres rivers, part of the country we now call Iraq.

---

transfer – To move something from one place to another.

---

value – The worth, importance or usefulness of something.

---

wealth – A large amount of money, property or other valuable things that a person has.

About the Author
Deborah Meaden is a highly-successful entrepreneur and one of Britain's best-known business names. Deborah has been an investor on *Dragon's Den* since 2006, and she also hosts BBC Radio 5 Live's *The Big Green Money*.

About the Illustrator
Based in Beijing, Hao Hao majored in stage design at the city's Central Academy of Drama, but her passion for painting has led to a highly successful career in illustration.